I'M ALLERGIC

I'M ALLERGIC TO BEES

By Kristen Rajczak

Gareth Stevens
PUBLISHING

Please visit our website, www.garethstevens.com. For a free color catalog of all our high-quality books, call toll free 1-800-542-2595 or fax 1-877-542-2596.

Library of Congress Cataloging-in-Publication Data

Rajczak, Kristen.
I'm allergic to bees / by Kristen Rajczak.
    p. cm. — (I'm allergic)
Includes index.
ISBN 978-1-4824-0788-4 (pbk.)
ISBN 978-1-4824-0967-3 (6-pack)
ISBN 978-1-4824-0787-7 (library binding)
1. Allergy in children — Juvenile literature. 2. Allergy — Juvenile literature. 3. Bees — Juvenile literature. I. Rajczak, Kristen. II. Title.
RC585.R35 2015
616.97—d23

Published in 2015 by
Gareth Stevens Publishing
111 East 14th Street, Suite 349
New York, NY 10003

Designer: Nicholas Domiano
Editor: Kristen Rajczak

Photo credits: cover, p. 1 (girl) © iStockphoto.com/eyespeakin; cover, p. 1 (bees) irin-k/ Shutterstock.com; pp. 3–24 (background texture), 11, 21 iStock/Thinkstock.com; p. 5 Jim H Walling/ Shutterstock.com; p. 7 Photodisc/Thinkstock.com; p. 9 Tyler Olson/Shutterstock.com; p. 13 W Treat Davidson/Photo Researchers/Getty Images; p. 15 Peter Dazeley/Photographer's Choice/Getty Images; p. 17 amanaimagesRF/Thinkstock.com; p. 19 (hornet) Barnaby Chambers/ Shutterstock.com; p. 19 (black wasp) alexsvirid/Shutterstock.com; p. 19 (bumblebee) Maksim Vivtsaruk/Shutterstock.com; p. 19 (yellow jacket) Paul Fell/Shutterstock.com.

Printed in the United States of America

CPSIA compliance information: Batch #CS15GS: For further information contact Gareth Stevens, New York, New York at 1-800-542-2595.

CONTENTS

Boldface words appear in the glossary.

Ouch!

Oh, no! While you were playing outside, a bee stung you. Bee stings hurt, but most of the time they're not dangerous. If you're allergic to bees, though, you need to get help right away!

Allergies

An allergy is the body's **reaction** to matter that's normally **harmless**. This matter is called an allergen (AA-luhr-juhn). The body treats it as an **intruder**. The body makes tiny allergen fighters called antibodies. Antibodies travel around your body in your blood.

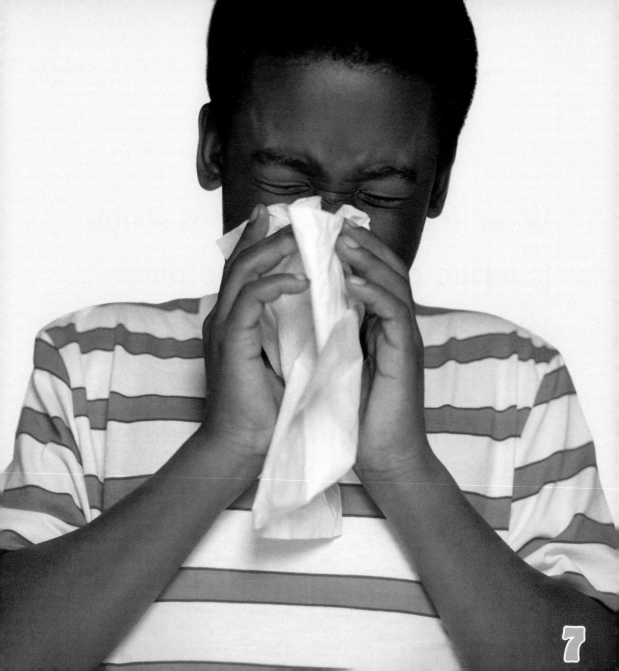

When a bee stings you, its stinger is pulled off its body and often left in your skin. It has a sac filled with **venom** that gets into your body. The venom is the allergen.

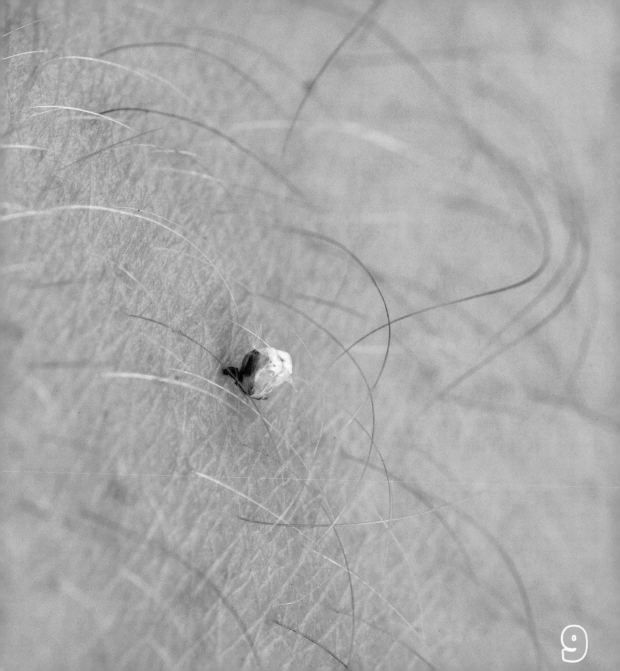

You've Been Stung!

Remove a bee stinger quickly so less venom has time to enter your body. Wash the sting with soap and water, and put ice on it. In normal reactions, the area will be red and may itch or ache a little.

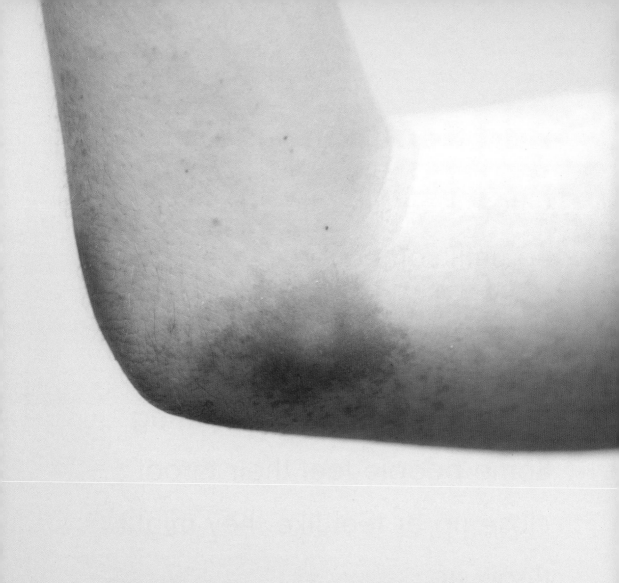

11

Bad Reaction

Often, bee allergies don't show up until someone has been stung more than once. An allergic reaction might include **hives**, trouble breathing, or **swelling**. Some people feel their throat close up or feel like they might throw up.

13

Very bad allergic reactions to bee stings cause anaphylaxis (aa-nuh-fuh-LAK-suhs). Anaphylaxis needs to be treated right away by a drug called epinephrine (eh-puh-NEH-fruhn). It's given as a shot—and sometimes people need more than one!

Doctors can test for bee allergies, but the tests aren't given unless someone has a reaction. Shots of very small amounts of bee venom given every week or month may **cure** the allergy. It takes many years to work, though.

Other Stingers

Other bugs that sting can cause allergic reactions, too. Yellow jackets, wasps, and hornets are all stinging bugs. People can be allergic to more than one of these bugs, too, so it's important to be careful around them all.

HORNET

YELLOW JACKET

BUMBLEBEE

BLACK WASP

19

Bee Careful

The best way to **prevent** allergic reactions to bee stings is to not get stung! Keep food covered when you're outside, especially sweets. If a bee is flying near you, don't run or swat it. Walk away calmly.

21

GLOSSARY

cure: to make healthy after an illness

harmless: unable to cause pain or injury

hives: raised, itchy patches of skin that are redder or paler than the skin around them

intruder: someone who forces their way into a place they're not wanted

prevent: to keep from happening

reaction: a response

swelling: getting bigger in an uncommon way

venom: something an animal makes in its body that can hurt other animals

FOR MORE INFORMATION

BOOKS

Rissman, Rebecca. *Bees*. Chicago, IL: Raintree, 2013.

Robbins, Lynette. *How to Deal with Allergies*. New York, NY: PowerKids Press, 2010.

WEBSITES

Allergies: From Bee Stings to Peanuts
www.sciencenewsforkids.org/2004/04/allergies-from-bee-stings-to-peanuts-2/
Read this article to find out more about bee, nut, and other common allergies.

Hey! A Bee Stung Me!
kidshealth.org/kid/watch/out/bee.html#cat20562
Learn more about bees, other stinging insects, and what to do if one stings you.

INDEX